Basics

For any professional musician, making music is all a matter of habits. From the way musicians stand or sit when they make music to the way they breathe and produce sound, everything they do is a carefully taught, finely disciplined habit.

One of your most important singing habits is that of good posture. Your posture affects your sound, because it affects the way you breathe. Your singing posture is important not only when you walk onstage to perform, but also when you're practicing, taking a lesson or coaching, or participating in a rehearsal. Rehearsals can be the most difficult places to maintain good posture, simply because you can't take a break to stretch or move around when you want to. By the end of a rehearsal you may be tired and you may have to fight to maintain good posture.

Good singing posture, whether sitting or standing, is relaxed, with a straight spine and neck. Hips are directly underneath the shoulders, with the pelvis neither tilted to the front or back. When standing, feet are shoulder width apart. When sitting, feet are flat on the floor.

Try the following breathing exercise using good and bad standing posture and good and bad sitting posture. You'll understand the importance of good posture immediately.

Placing one hand on your chest and one on your abdomen, exhale slowly until your lungs feel quite empty. Now inhale three times, without exhaling in between, thinking about filling up your lungs in thirds. After the last breath, you lungs should feel quite full. Take two quick inhales through your nose, which should give you a feeling of being slightly overfull of air. Exhale slowly and gently, relaxing as you do so. This is a great exercise to add to daily and pre-gig warm-ups.

In Goes the Good Air

Singers talk a lot about breathing from the diaphragm and about supporting their sound. Although you never want your diaphragm control to be a tense, rigid process, you do need to know where your diaphragm is and what it feels like when it's working.

To locate your diaphragm and to wake it up, place you hand on your abdomen and utter a loud, indignant "Hah!" Go ahead, really make a statement with it. You should feel you diaphragm work to expel a blast of air for the "Hah."

Now let's put the breath support we've been practicing to use on actual notes. Stand, with your hand on abdomen. Sing the octaves shown below, starting on a pitch that is comfortable in your range. When the high octave starts to feel like you're reaching for it, stop and sing them in reverse, high note to low note. Your hand will feel your diaphragm working differently for the low and high notes. It can also help you stay relaxed and make the shifts from low to high and from high to low both smoothly and easily.

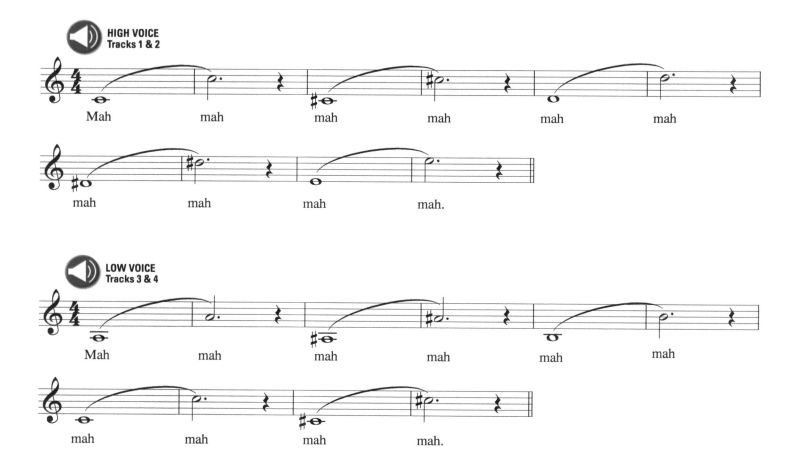

For all the exercises in this book: Sopranos and tenors should begin with the high-voice vocalises; altos and baritones should begin with the low-voice vocalises. As you progress and as your vocal range increases, you may wish to do both sets of exercises. However, if an exercise gets too high or too low for you, if your throat feels tight, if you start straining, or if you can't hit the note, just stop and use the range (high or low) that is comfortable. After some work, you might be able to go higher or lower. Remember, everyone's voice is different. Develop yours to its unique potential.

Hold That Note

Your diaphragm is the engine that powers your voice. It moves air in and out of your lungs and allows you to sing without damaging your voice. Repeat the "hah" exercise from page 4 to wake up your diaphragm. In this exercise you are going to work on controlling the flow of air from your lungs without tensing the diaphragm.

To work on relaxed, even breath control, stand up, let your arms hang loose at your sides and take a deep, soothing breath. Exhale on a very soft, controlled "sss" sound, until you need to breathe again. It's not as easy as it sounds. When you first begin doing this exercise, you are likely to notice that the "sss" sound is uneven and sometimes shaky. Don't tense up – it won't help. Do it again, always with a deep, relaxed inhale and soft steady "sss" sound. The more you work on this, the easier it gets.

Needless to say, not all music you sing will require a soft, delicate sound. You can work on even, relaxed breath support for a big, full sound by doing the same exercise with a big, full "sss" sound as well. Once again, work to make it perfectly smooth, with no wobbles or lurches. You will not be able to sustain the loud "sss" as long as you could sustain the soft one.

After a week or two of working on the "sss" sound, add a hum to this exercise. Start by adding a *mf* (medium loud) hum. Once you have smoothed the bumps out at that dynamic (it may take several weeks of including this in your warm-ups to make it as smooth as you would like), work on making a steady hum in all dynamics.

Ups & Downs

If you've never used the useless term "pitchy," good for you. If you have used it, stop doing so immediately. Faltering or wavering pitch is clear indicator of vocal/musical weakness. Musical notes can be perfectly in tune, which is always the goal, or they can be sharp (a bit too high), or flat (a bit too low). Either way, wandering pitch needs to be fixed. For singers, this means learning to hear whether you're sharp or flat and learning to make subtle adjustments.

A great way to help you hear pitch more accurately is to do a simple "slide" exercise between notes. Pick either the high voice or low voice "slide" recording on the audio that accompanies this book. You will be singing the first five notes of a major scale, first ascending then descending, sliding from one to the next.

The recording will give you a starting note, which you will match and sustain. When the note on the audio changes, slide to that note and sustain it, matching the pitch of the note you hear. Stop when the note on the audio stops. The note you just matched will sound again. Match it and sustain it. When it changes, slide to the note you hear and match it. Repeat this until you have sung the first five notes of the scale and then repeat the process descending back to the starting note.

When you begin working on this exercise, you may find yourself sliding too far or not far enough, and then overcorrecting. It may not be a pretty process. But in the space of a few days of doing this exercise, you should begin to develop pitch accuracy.

Fine Tuning

This is a more advanced version of the sliding exercise you just learned. It is designed to develop pitch and interval accuracy within a major scale. Just like the previous exercise, a note will sound and you will match and sustain it. When the note changes, you will slide to that note, sustaining it and holding strictly in tune. Stop when that note stops and wait for the tonic of the scale to sound again. Match it and wait for the note shift and then slide to that note and repeat the process with the recording until you have worked on the entire octave. Once you have mastered the ascending scale slides, work on the descending slides.

Don't worry if this is slow going at first, or if some of the intervals are harder to hear and sing than others. All of this is perfectly normal and will disappear with repetition.

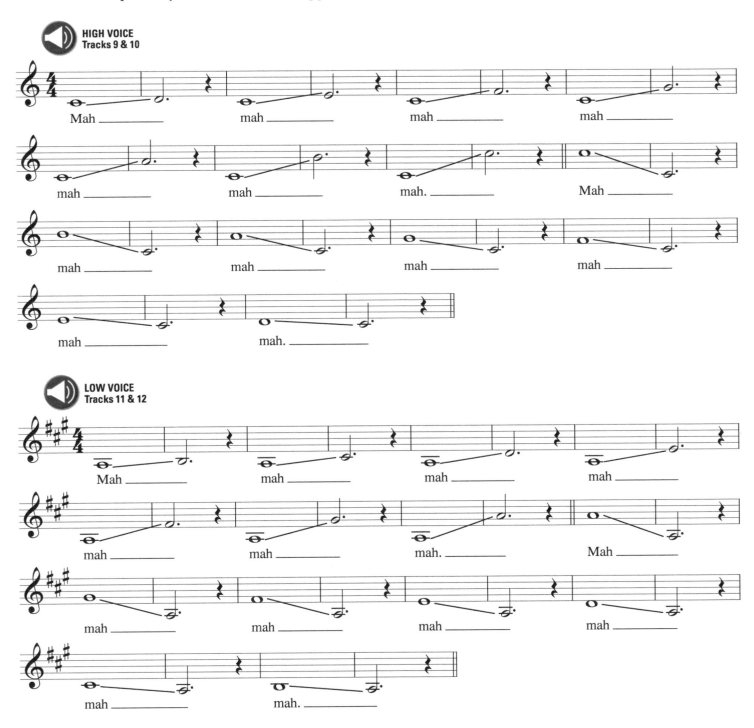

HIGH VOICE
Tracks 9 & 10

LOW VOICE
Tracks 11 & 12

An Interval by Any Other Name

Now that you have worked on developing interval accuracy within a major scale, it's a good time to develop a little musical literacy to go along with that accuracy. There's nothing quite so confidence-destroying as having someone tell you that your perfect fourth was a little flat and having no idea what they're talking about.

This exercise is a simple learning-by-repetition drill. You will be singing a major scale in intervals, first using solfège (do-re-mi, etc.) and then using the interval names. The exercise will teach and then reinforce the names and distances of the intervals within the scale.

Just as was the case with the sliding exercise, don't worry if this is slow going at first, or if some of the intervals are harder to hear and sing than others. All of this is perfectly normal and will disappear with repetition.

HIGH VOICE
Tracks 13 & 14

LOW VOICE
Tracks 15 & 16

Digital Ears

A great way to help you hear and control pitch variations is to work with a digital tuner. Although many singers think of them as tools for instrumentalists only, that's not the case. You can pick up a good digital tuner for under 20 dollars, or you can download a good, smart phone tuner app for just a few bucks.

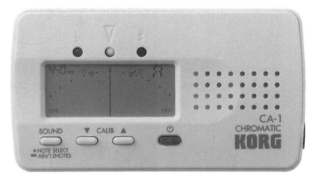

Turn on the tuner and play with it for a few minutes. You can sing a line of a favorite song or just sing a scale. Notice how sensitive the tuner is to any variations in pitch.

To start working with it, choose a note that sits lower than the center of your range and sing it into the tuner, striving to center the "needle" that registers pitch variations. Now sing the first five notes of the major scale, ascending and descending, as shown below for high voice and low voice and as provided on audio tracks 17 and 18.

Sing these notes slowly, watching the tuner and listening to your pitch as you sing. Tuners can be frustrating tools, particularly when you first start working with them. Don't be discouraged and don't work for very long on this. As you come back to this day after and day, you will see progress in your sense of pitch and your understanding of intervals.

HIGH VOICE
Track 17

LOW VOICE
Track 18

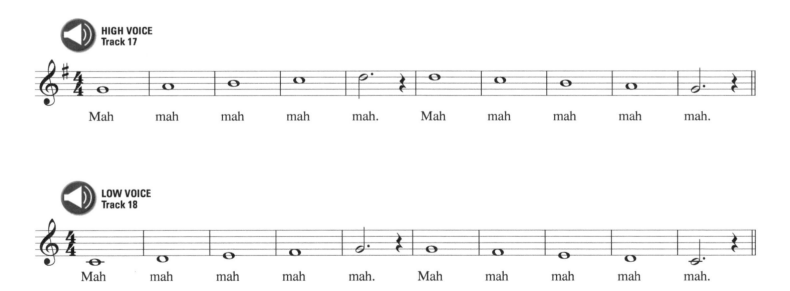

Short & Sweet

Curiously enough, just as sliding is great for developing pitch accuracy and command, so is staccato singing. Sing "The House of the Rising Sun" as written. Once you are comfortable with the melody, sing it as though each note were marked staccato (short or separated), using the syllable "mah" for each note. The object of this kind of practice is to center on the pitch immediately, with no wavering or scooping. Use this technique with any song you're learning to work on pitch accuracy and the confidence it brings.

The House of the Rising Sun
Southern American Folk Song

Tracks 19 & 20

Details, Details

This exercise uses your digital tuner or the tuner app on your phone, to work on fine control of a single pitch – in other words, rising and sinking just a bit on a single note. This control is an absolute must as you perform.

Turn on your tuner and pick a pitch somewhere in the middle of your range. Sustain the pitch and work on centering the "needle" on the tuner or tuner app. In other words, bring the pitch in tune with your tuner. Stop and restart the note several times, working on hitting it spot on at the beginning of the note. Once you are comfortable starting the note accurately, work on raising and lowering the "needle" slowly and smoothly. You will be changing the pitch in tiny increments, which is exactly the point. Concentrate on making the "needle" of your tuner move just a little bit and making it move without jumps and lurches. This exercise can be frustrating at first, so don't work on it too much in a single session. This kind of fine pitch control takes a while to develop, so be patient.

Dressing Up Your Sound with Vibrato

Think of vibrato as a scarf or necktie used to put a finishing touch on a dressy outfit or suit and you can't go wrong. Think of it as a uniform that you wear at all times and you will most certainly go very wrong. Basically, if you can't sing without vibrato, you shouldn't be singing with it.

You can sing with or without vibrato, as the music indicates and as your taste dictates. You can add a faster, more dramatic vibrato to a loud, high passage, and a slow, easy vibrato to something that is low and soft. You can speed up your vibrato and slow it down and you can hold a note without vibrato and then add it near the end.

Vibrato is a natural part of musical sound and it develops quite naturally when a singer, or wind or brass player, uses a well-supported stream of air. The way to learn how to use vibrato is to listen to other singers who are singing the same genre of music you are working on. You don't want to bring an operatic vibrato to a country tune or a folk music vibrato to an art song. Listen to singers and pay attention to the details of vibrato. When it is used well, it brings color, warmth, and drama to music.

To work on your own vibrato, pick a note in the comfortable middle of your range and work on sustaining it with no vibrato at all. Then work on adding vibrato at the end of the note. Then try using vibrato throughout the note. As you get comfortable using and not using vibrato, move closer to the outer limits of your range and work on adding a fast vibrato to high notes and slower vibrato to low notes

Like a singer's voice itself, vibrato varies from singer to singer. There is no one-size-fits-all vibrato. There is a difference, however, between using vibrato well and using it poorly.

Dynamite Dynamics

Vocal strength is not limited to the ability to sing loudly. But having a wide range of dynamics under your control and ready to use is most certainly a part of strong singing.

A good way to start building your dynamic range is to sing long tones with a crescendo or a diminuendo. Listen to the singers on the demo tracks and then sing along with the accompaniment tracks. In addition to simply getting louder and softer, listen carefully to make sure you are not drifting sharp or flat in the process. Work on making your crescendos and diminuendos perfectly smooth, growing louder and softer in a graceful arc.

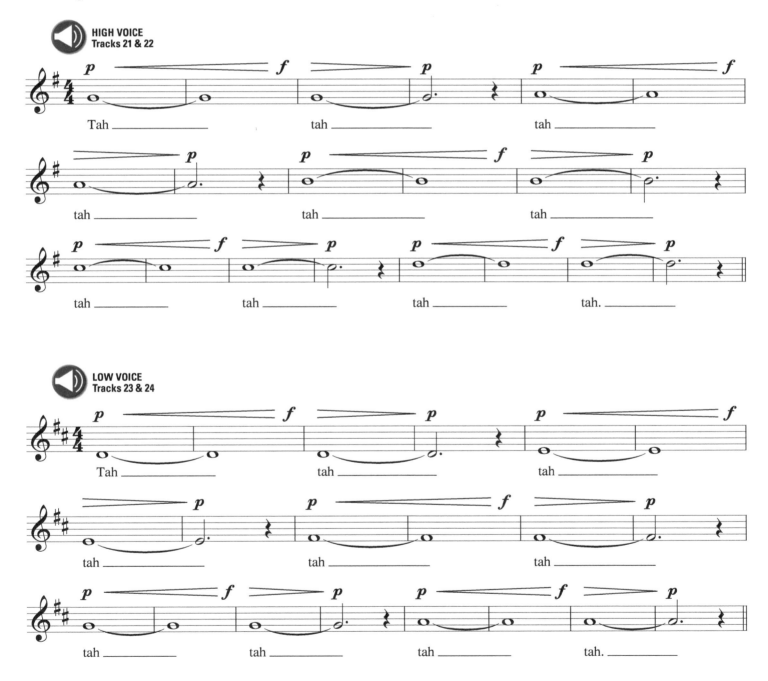

Taking Dynamics Out for a Spin

A very wise teacher once told me that when a performer steps onstage, he or she can count on shaving 10 to 15 percent off of the best rendition they've done of whatever it is they're performing. Perhaps it's nerves, perhaps it the sense of caution that overcomes a lot of performers when they see an audience. Whatever it is, some of the best moments of musical and technical artistry you created in a practice room or in rehearsals are likely to pale a bit in front of an audience. To counteract this tendency to hold back, always practice with the idea of *more* in your head. Do larger crescendos and diminuendos than you really intend to do in performance. Do more *rubato* than you actually will use on stage. Enunciate more than you would in front of an audience, and so on.

In Exercise 11 you worked to achieve Dynamite Dynamics. Now use the following song to overstate crescendos on each phrase, then do it again with diminuendos on each phrase. Sing the entire song at a *forte* dynamic and then sing it again at a *piano* dynamic. Listen to the singer on Track 25 give you a polished performance.

Look for the Silver Lining

from *Sally*

Words by Buddy DeSylva
Music by Jerome Kern

Tracks 25 & 26

Keys to Success

Transposition is your friend. A great way to work on expanding your range in small, safe increments, as well as solidifying your sense of relative pitch (basically making intervals secure and in tune regardless of what key you're in), is transposing the melody you're singing.

A simple folksong, "Russian Lullaby," is shown below in the key of C major (Tracks 27 & 28). Work on it for a few days and get comfortable with the melody and tempo. Once you know it, sing it in D major (Track 29). It's been transposed up only a major second, but it will feel quite different from the first key. After several days of working on the tune in D major, move on to Track 30 and work on it in E major for a few days. Then return to the original key. For most singers, transposing music for practice solidifies the pitches and intervals within the song and increases their comfort with the song. As always, feeling comfortable with a song and in command as you sing keeps tension to a minimum.

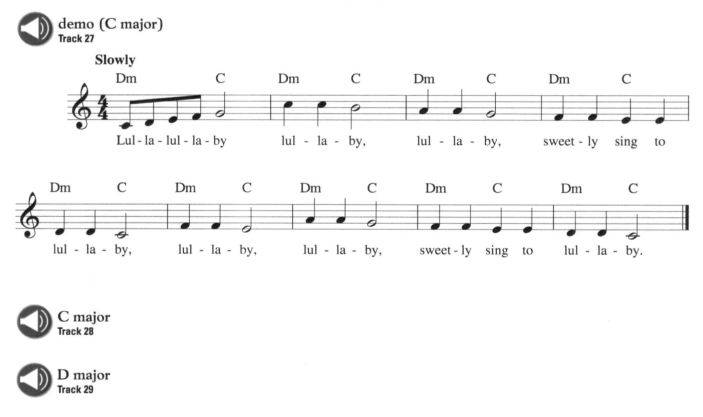

demo (C major)
Track 27

C major
Track 28

D major
Track 29

E major
Track 30

You can transpose anything you're working on simply by starting a whole step higher or lower than the note on which the song or phrase begins. Once you're comfortable in that key area, take another step in the same direction. Always work on it a day or two before moving another step or returning to the original key.

Facilitating Facility

Some of the songs you work on will be slow and legato, meant to be crooned. But others will be fast and full of moving notes. Think of "Supercalifragilisticexpialidocious" from *Mary Poppins*, for instance. Or better yet, do a web search for "I Am the Very Model of a Modern Major General" from the operetta *The Pirates of Penzance*. Aside from the issue of simply learning the words, imagine singing that tune up to tempo.

Vocal facility, or the ability to sing notes quickly and accurately, is an achievable goal. Like any other technical vocal skill, you must start out slowly and build speed as you become more competent. You may switch syllables to "lah" or "mah" over time. Once you have really mastered the exercise and have it up to a brisk tempo, transpose it higher or lower in your vocal range and master it there as well. By alternating the middle, high, and lower areas of your range with this exercise, you will develop facility and control throughout your range.

HIGH VOICE
Tracks 31 & 32

Tah tah tah tah   *etc.*

LOW VOICE
Tracks 33 & 34

Tah tah tah tah   *etc.*

Strong Body, Strong Sound

Supporting your sound with steady stream of air is essential to making a clear, consistent, relaxed sound. A real help is creating that kind of air support is developing strong muscles in your body's core. This does not mean doing endless series of crunches and shooting for perfect "six-pack" abs – although more power to you if you want to do that. A more realistic goal for most people is developing core strength through something like yoga or Pilates, or through some simple, daily exercises that target the muscles that surround the core of the torso – and that does mean the muscles on the sides and back of the torso, not just the abs. Planking and bridging are two no-impact exercises that have become popular in recent years. As always, check with your doctor before embarking on any training or exercise program.

For **planking**, lie on your stomach on the floor. Raise your head and shoulders by resting your weight on your forearms and place your feet as though you're about to do push-ups. Raise up your body until you're back is straight as a plank of wood, and support yourself in this position for three counts before gently lowering body to your starting position. If you can support yourself in this fashion for more than three counts, that's great. Do it. The goal is to increase the time you support yourself in the plank position. Try adding a count every few days to increase your endurance and, with it, your core muscle strength.

For **bridging**, lie on your back, arms at your sides and knees sharply bent, with feet close to your bottom, about shoulder width apart. Push up, so that your knees, torso, and shoulders form a straight line and hold for three (or more) counts. Repeat several times. Try to hold for one additional count every few days.

Take a Hike

Walking is a fabulous and free form of exercise. When you walk, particularly at a brisk pace, you work your core muscles, your legs, and your cardiovascular system. You can walk indoors or outdoors, rain or shine. You can set aside long periods for long walks and fit short walks into small time slots. You can incorporate more walking into your daily life simply by parking an extra block or so from every place you go in a given day.

You can listen to music you are learning as you walk, although **be careful** and **stay alert** if you do. Listening to music on an mp3 player while walking is the cause of many unfortunate accidents. You can work on lyrics while you walk simply by chanting the lyrics to the constant beat of your footfalls, or do the same with rhythms by chanting the rhythms of a song to your footfalls.

Remember, any cardiovascular exercise (walking, swimming, running, biking, etc.) increases your breath control and endurance, and therefore your vocal strength.

To Thine Own Self Be True

No two voices are the same. Even voices that can be described in similar terms, such as two country tenors or two classical sopranos, can really be quite different from one another. Some of the differences are interpretive, but some lie purely in the singer's sounds. Paul McCartney and Elton John are both tenors, both British, and both are famous rock musicians, yet you would never confuse the two.

Never try to force your voice into someone else's mold. Much of a singer's distinctive sound is created by that person's unique physical attributes. Your sound is going to be your own. You can study and practice vocal technique to strengthen and polish your sound and you can work with a coach to shape your musical deliveries. You can even do careful work to gently expand your range a bit, but your sound is pretty well determined for you.

No matter what your voice type or preferred style of music, you need to be able to use your voice fluently to make the best possible sound and to be able to make meaningful musical statements. Sometimes simple lines, which have to be solidly supported, smoothly connected, and artfully shaped can be the hardest things to sing well. They can reveal a host of the singer's strengths and weaknesses.

Work on singing the African-American spiritual "Sometimes I Feel Like a Motherless Child" with a smooth, easy sound and fluid connections between the notes within each phrase. Once you have mastered the technical aspects or the tune, shape the phrases using dynamics (changes in volume) to give them meaning. It's always good to have a song like this in your proverbial back pocket to take you from warming up to making music.

Sometimes I Feel Like a Motherless Child

African-American Spiritual

Arpeggios

Pianos, guitars, organs, and other harmonic instruments (instruments that can play more than one note at a time) can play chords. Singers cannot produce more than one note at a time, but can sing through chords one note at a time, turning them into arpeggios. Arpeggios pop up in a great deal of the music we sing, outlining harmony and giving a broad, sweeping feeling to the vocal lines of songs.

Listen to the singers in Tracks 37 and 39, as they move through this arpeggio warm-up. Tracks 38 and 40 contain just the high- and low-voice accompaniments for these warm-ups. When working on these exercises, always strive for accurate pitch and an even sound from the bottom to the top of the arpeggios. You may extend this exercise either higher or lower on your vocal range for more of a workout from top to bottom.

In addition to "lah," you can use the following syllables:
- mah
- mih
- too

Exercise 19

Baby Steps

We've worked on major scale intervals, on octaves and on arpeggios, but we haven't worked on the smallest of intervals, the half step. Half steps, which form the basis for the chromatic scale, can be particularly tricky to sing in tune. The interval between the notes is small, making it very easy to overshoot.

Work on the following exercises, which you can listen to on Track 41. The accompaniment appears on Track 42. Work slowly and carefully, making sure to match the pitches you hear on the accompaniment track. As always, start out slowly and speed it up over time.

Tracks 41 & 42

Next, work on applying your half-step accuracy to "I Ain't Got Nobody" on page 24.

I Ain't Got Nobody
(And Nobody Cares for Me)

Words by Roger Graham
Music by Spencer Williams and Dave Peyton

24

Exercise 20

Diction

Song lyrics matter. More to the point, communicating those lyrics to your audience matters. Actors and public speakers keep a list of tongue twisters that they use to warm up the tongue and facial musicals to ensure intelligible diction when they are performing or speaking. For singers, clear diction helps prevent the over-singing and muscle tension that stems from struggling to be understood.

If you have a specific set of consonants and/or vowels that are difficult for you to say in quick succession, do a web search for tongue twisters and find one that works those issues. Sing them to a scale, just as the following exercises are sung.

Sing these tongue twisters, slowly at first, until they are comfortable and clearly enunciated. Then begin to speed them up gradually. Have fun with this one. (On the sing-along tracks, each exercise is played four times: intro, slow, medium, fast.)

Practice Songs

Both "Danny Boy" and "Hard Times Come Again No More" have been part of the English language folk tradition for more than a century. Learn these songs in as they appear on the page, following the notes and rhythms strictly. Once you know the songs well, you can begin to work on your own interpretations.

Tracks 57 & 58

Danny Boy

        Track 57   Demo

        Track 58   Sing-Along

Tracks 59 & 60

Hard Times Come Again No More

        Track 59   Demo

        Track 60   Sing-Along

Danny Boy

Words by Frederick Edward Weatherly
Traditional Irish Folk Melody

Hard Times Come Again No More

Words and Music by Stephen C. Foster

pro vocal®
BETTER THAN KARAOKE!

Whether you're a karaoke singer or an auditioning professional, the **Pro Vocal®** series is for you! Unlike most karaoke packs, each book in the Pro Vocal series contains the lyrics, melody, and chord symbols for at least eight hit songs. The audio contains demos for listening, and separate backing tracks so you can sing along. Perfect for home rehearsal, parties, auditions, corporate events, and gigs without a backup band.

WOMEN'S EDITIONS

MEN'S EDITIONS

EXERCISES

MIXED EDITIONS

These editions feature songs for both male and female voices.

KIDS EDITIONS

Visit Hal Leonard online at
www.halleonard.com

HAL•LEONARD®

Prices, contents, & availability subject to change without notice.
Disney Characters and Artwork TM & © 2018 Disney

HAL LEONARD BROADWAY VOCAL SELECTIONS

     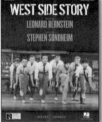 

00313506	The Addams Family	$19.99
00313175	Aida	$19.99
00359040	Ain't Misbehavin'	$19.99
00126656	Aladdin	$19.99
00313301	All Shook Up	$19.99
00156237	Amazing Grace	$17.99
00241528	Amélie	$17.99
00148752	An American in Paris	$17.99
00197874	Anastasia	$19.99
00383056	Annie	$16.99
00005576	Annie Get Your Gun	$12.99
00312010	Anyone Can Whistle	$11.99
00313269	Avenue Q	$24.99
00276002	The Band's Visit	$19.99
00313355	Barnum	$16.95
00250379	Be More Chill	$17.99
00123827	Beautiful (Carole King)	$19.99
00313194	The Beautiful Game	$17.95
00312511	Beauty and the Beast	$22.99
00302238	Beetlejuice	$22.99
00125618	Big Fish	$19.99
00359270	Big River	$17.99
00313432	Billy Elliot	$22.99
00138578	The Bridges of Madison County	$24.99
00313469	Brigadoon	$17.99
00175428	Bright Star	$19.99
00119255	Bring It On	$19.99
00251958	A Bronx Tale	$17.99
00313310	Brooklyn	$14.95
00313233	Bye, Bye Birdie	$19.99
00294998	Calendar Girls	$14.99
00450014	Candide	$16.99
01121002	Carmen Jones	$16.99
02502276	Caroline, Or Change	$19.99
01121008	Carousel	$16.99
00119339	Carrie	$22.99
00359466	Cats	$17.99
00117502	Chaplin	$16.99
00251959	Charlie and the Chocolate Factory	$17.99
00123037	Chess	$16.99
00312087	Chicago	$16.99
00313326	Children of Eden	$17.99
00383312	A Chorus Line	$17.99
00312091	Cinderella (Original)	$17.99
00119879	Cinderella on Broadway	$19.99
00313356	City of Angels	$16.95
02500261	The Civil War	$19.99
00313364	The Color Purple	$17.99
00313497	Come Fly Away	$19.99
00250241	Come from Away	$19.99
00359494	Company	$19.99
00313384	Curtains	$19.99
00226474	Dear Evan Hansen	$22.99
00313490	Dreamgirls	$17.99

00313361	The Drowsy Chaperone	$19.99
00313463	End of the Rainbow	$16.99
00120566	Evita	$16.99
00359861	Fiddler on the Roof	$17.99
00201020	Finding Neverland	$16.99
00123635	First Date	$17.99
00312140	Flower Drum Song	$14.95
00313306	Follies	$29.99
00313608	Footloose	$17.99
00313473	The Frogs	$17.99
00281007	Frozen	$19.99
00313222	The Full Monty	$14.95
00312151	A Funny Thing Happened on the Way to the Forum	$12.99
00125464	A Gentleman's Guide to Love and Murder	$16.99
00313633	Ghost	$19.99
00359902	Godspell	$17.99
02500734	Grand Hotel	$14.95
00383675	Grease	$17.99
00313365	Grey Gardens	$17.99
00283919	Groundhog Day	$19.99
00446425	Guys & Dolls	$19.99
00313249	Gypsy	$19.99
00313219	Hairspray	$22.99
00155921	Hamilton	$24.99
00313258	Hedwig & the Angry Inch	$17.99
00383730	Hello, Dolly!	$15.99
00194941	Holiday Inn	$17.99
00146103	Honeymoon in Vegas	$16.99
00383780	House of Flowers	$12.99
00446479	How to Succeed in Business Without Really Trying	$15.99
00234732	The Hunchback of Notre Dame	$19.99
00313140	I Love You, You're Perfect, Now Change	$19.99
00129555	If/Then	$16.99
00313411	In the Heights	$19.99
00313442	Into the Woods	$19.99
00153584	It Shoulda Been You	$17.99
00313415	It's Only Life	$16.95
00312047	Jacques Brel Is Alive & Well & Living in Paris	$19.99
00334355	Jagged Little Pill	$24.99
00119278	Jekyll & Hyde	$17.99
00313335	Jersey Boys	$17.99
00123602	Jesus Christ Superstar	$17.99
00251079	John & Jen	$19.99
00312505	Joseph and the Amazing Technicolor Dreamcoat	$19.99
00312227	The King and I	$17.99
00313277	Kiss of the Spider Woman	$19.99
00384040	La Cage Aux Folles	$17.99
00313206	The Last Five Years	$19.99
00313421	Legally Blonde	$17.99
00360286	Les Misérables	$22.99

00313307	Light in the Piazza	$19.99
00259008	The Lightning Thief	$19.99
00313097	The Lion King	$19.99
00313402	The Little Mermaid	$22.99
00313478	A Little Night Music	$19.99
00313390	A Little Princess	$19.99
02500830	Little Women	$24.99
00313071	Louisiana Purchase	$10.95
00276502	Love Never Dies	$19.99
00384205	Mack and Mabel	$17.99
00384226	Mame	$16.99
00299480	The Man in the Ceiling	$19.99
02503701	Man of La Mancha	$16.99
00313303	Mary Poppins	$17.99
14042140	Matilda	$19.99
00287380	Mean Girls	$22.99
00313503	Memphis	$17.99
00313481	Merrily, We Roll Along	$17.99
00313535	Million Dollar Quartet	$16.99
00236351	Miss Saigon	$19.99
00121881	Motown	$16.99
00350573	Moulin Rouge	$19.99
00446752	The Music Man	$17.99
00312290	My Fair Lady	$14.99
00313275	The Mystery of Edwin Drood	$16.99
00313157	Myths and Hymns	$22.99
14048350	Natasha, Pierre & The Great Comet of 1812	$19.99
00124376	Night with Janis Joplin	$16.99
02502895	Nine	$19.99
00313498	9 to 5	$19.99
00122181	Now. Here. This.	$16.99
00312292	Oklahoma!	$17.99
00378806	Oliver!	$14.99
00312300	Once upon a Mattress	$15.99
00312310	Paint Your Wagon	$17.99
00233588	The Pajama Game	$17.99
00312313	Pal Joey	$16.99
00313148	Parade	$19.99
00313425	Passing Strange	$16.99
00384551	Peter Pan	$12.99
00360830	Phantom of the Opera	$22.99
00313376	The Pirate Queen	$17.95
00004034	The Pirates of Penzance	$10.99
00287171	Pretty Woman	$19.99
00349316	The Prince of Egypt	$19.99
00313591	Priscilla, Queen of the Desert	$16.99
00313189	The Producers	$24.99
00289027	The Prom	$19.99
00313232	Rags	$14.95
00322474	Ragtime	$24.99
00313069	Rent	$22.99
00313279	The Rink	$12.95
00313156	The Roar of the Greasepaint the Smell of the Crowd	$12.99

00313460	Rock of Ages	$24.99
00126814	Rocky	$16.99
14042919	Rocky Horror Show	$19.99
00313107	Saturday Night	$14.95
00158983	School of Rock	$19.99
02500764	Scrooge	$22.99
00311588	Secret Garden	$19.99
00313274	1776	$17.99
00313320	She Loves Me	$16.99
00313015	Show Boat	$16.99
02501371	Shrek	$24.99
00313096	Side Show	$22.99
00319800	Six	$19.99
00313080	Smokey Joe's Cafe	$17.99
00151276	Something Rotten!	$19.99
00313188	Songs for a New World	$17.99
00312392	The Sound of Music	$17.99
00312400	South Pacific	$16.99
00313302	Spamalot	$19.99
00313644	Spider-Man	$17.99
00313379	Spring Awakening	$22.99
00384828	A Star Is Born	$12.99
00312403	State Fair	$14.95
00378808	Stop the World – I Want to Get Off	$12.99
00312514	Sunset Boulevard	$19.99
00190369	The Theory of Relativity	$19.99
00313435	13	$24.99
02500565	Thoroughly Modern Millie	$19.99
00313197	tick, tick ... BOOM!	$19.99
02502216	Titanic	$22.99
00313455	[title of show]	$17.99
00313286	Tommy	$19.99
00299799	Tootsie	$19.99
00190505	Tuck Everlasting	$17.99
00447210	Unsinkable Molly Brown	$17.99
00313260	Urinetown	$19.99
00130743	Violet	$16.99
00204751	Waitress	$19.99
00249705	War Paint	$17.99
02500975	The Wedding Singer	$22.99
00450068	West Side Story	$19.99
00313429	White Christmas	$17.99
00313267	Wicked	$24.99
00313162	The Wild Party	$19.99
00313298	The Woman in White	$17.99
00740595	You're a Good Man, Charlie Brown	$16.99
00313404	Young Frankenstein	$24.99

HAL•LEONARD®

View songlists and browse even more vocal selections at **halleonard.com**

1220
477

ORIGINAL KEYS FOR SINGERS

Titles in the Original Keys for Singers series are designed for vocalists looking for authentic transcriptions from their favorite artists. The books transcribe famous vocal performances exactly as recorded and provide piano accompaniment parts so that you can perform or pratice exactly as Ella or Patsy or Josh!

ACROSS THE UNIVERSE
00307010..$19.95

ADELE
00155395..$19.99

LOUIS ARMSTRONG
00307029..$19.99

THE BEATLES
00307400..$19.99

BROADWAY HITS (FEMALE SINGERS)
00119085..$19.99

BROADWAY HITS (MALE SINGERS)
00119084..$19.99

PATSY CLINE
00740072..$22.99

ELLA FITZGERALD
00740252..$22.99

JOSH GROBAN
00306969..$19.99

BILLIE HOLIDAY
Transcribed from Historic Recordings
00740140..$19.99

ETTA JAMES: GREATEST HITS
00130427..$19.99

JAZZ DIVAS
00114959..$19.99

LADIES OF CHRISTMAS
00312192..$19.99

NANCY LAMOTT
00306995..$19.99

MEN OF CHRISTMAS
00312241..$19.99

THE BETTE MIDLER SONGBOOK
00307067..$19.99

THE BEST OF LIZA MINNELLI
00306928..$19.99

ONCE
00102569..$16.99

ELVIS PRESLEY
00138200..$19.99

SHOWSTOPPERS FOR FEMALE SINGERS
00119640..$19.99

BEST OF NINA SIMONE
00121576..$19.99

FRANK SINATRA – MORE OF HIS BEST
00307081..$19.99

TAYLOR SWIFT
00142702..$16.99

SARAH VAUGHAN
00306558..$24.99

VOCAL POP
00312656..$19.99

ANDY WILLIAMS – CHRISTMAS COLLECTION
00307158..$17.99

ANDY WILLIAMS
00307160..$17.99

HAL•LEONARD®
www.halleonard.com

Prices, contents, and availability subject to change without notice.

Building Vocal Strength

Vocal strength is essential to producing a good sound, singing with control and confidence, as well as singing for many years. A weak voice is one that tires easily, one that is inconsistent in sound quality and/or pitch and dynamics, and one that gives out many years before the singer is ready to stop singing. Vocal strength is not all about singing loudly. It's about singing well.

The exercises and musical selections in this book are designed to help singers hone and refine their skills to develop the kind of control and consistency professional singers need to compete and find work. But mastering these skills is not just a task for professional singers – amateur singers who work on the exercises in this book will find singing easier and more fun with each new level of control they achieve.

These exercises are intended to be added to an existing daily vocal warm-up routine, one at a time. Once you have mastered the skill in the exercise, keep the exercise in your warm-up routine, but work on it a few times a week, rather than daily. As you finish with one, begin on another, which you will also take to an a-few-times-a-week status after you've mastered it.

The walking and core strengthening exercises can remain part of your everyday routine – whether or not you practice on that given day.

Vocal strength means endurance, no tension, breath control, technical control, fluidity/facility – basically ease in everything you do as a singer.

After you've made your way through the book, you may want to pick and choose a few of the exercises that are particularly helpful to music you're performing and include them in your pre-gig warm-up routine.

HAL•LEONARD

Pro Vocal
BETTER THAN KARAOKE!

VOCAL EXERCISES

PLAYBACK+
Speed • Pitch • Balance • Loop

To access audio visit:
www.halleonard.com/mylibrary

8082-2986-5325-4124

Text by Elaine Schmidt
Tracking, mixing, and mastering by Ric Probst at Remote Planet, Milwaukee
Vocals: Beth Mulkerron & Jesse Weinberg; Piano: J. Mark Baker

ISBN 978-1-4803-6564-3

HAL•LEONARD®
CORPORATION

7777 W. BLUEMOUND RD. P.O. BOX 13819 MILWAUKEE, WI 53213

In Australia Contact:
Hal Leonard Australia Pty. Ltd.
4 Lentara Court
Cheltenham, Victoria, 3192 Australia
Email: ausadmin@halleonard.com.au

Visit Hal Leonard Online at
www.halleonard.com